What is my **horse** thinking?

What is my **horse** thinking?

LESLEY BAYLEY

hamlyn

First published in Great Britain in 2002 by
Hamlyn, a division of Octopus Publishing Group Limited
2–4 Heron Quays, London E14 4JP

Distributed in the United States and Canada by
Sterling Publishing Co., Inc.
387 Park Avenue South, New York, NY 10016-8810

ISBN 0 600 60485 3

A CIP catalogue record for this book is available from the British Library

Printed and bound in China

10 9 8 7 6 5 4 3 2 1

Contents

INTRODUCTION   6

HORSES IN THE FIELD   8

HORSES IN THE STABLE   36

RIDING   54

TRAINING   68

TRAVELLING   88

INDEX   94

Introduction

Horse watching is a fascinating pastime and one that can take up many pleasurable hours. There are many different breeds of horses, from majestic heavy horses such as Shires and Percherons to fine-boned speed merchants such as Thoroughbreds and Arabs. In between are many mountain and moorland types like Exmoors and Highlands, hardy, distinctive animals like Haflingers and Norwegian Fjords, and horses with distinct actions like Hackneys and Tennessee Walkers.

Whichever country a horse comes from, his language is universal. Russian horses meeting American Morgans can communicate – for horses use body language, touch, smell and sound to 'talk' to other horses. If we can understand the signals they send out, we too can listen in on the conversations.

Horses are already tuning in to our thoughts and emotions: they are adept at reading our body language and will pick up on the slightest hesitation or doubt we might have. We may think that we are studying the horse's behaviour, but he is also watching us!

Whether a draught horse or a racehorse, a pet or a working animal, all horses still have a wild horse living inside them. Their natural instincts, the behaviour that has been programmed into them and has allowed them to survive to date, are never very far below the surface of any horse.

It is a great compliment to the adaptability of horses that they have lived to survive in the humans' world, where we make so many strange requests of them, often without even considering how peculiar these must be when seen through a horse's eyes.

Most of the problems people experience with their horses spring from a failure to consider the basic differences between ourselves and horses. We are predators and they are prey animals – so they are often simply doing their best to survive when they refuse to load into a trailer or walk into a river, run away from a large vehicle, do not want to have their feet picked up and so on. Horses are just being horses – they do not have human motives such as revenge and do not deliberately try to make life awkward for their owners.

A horse always has a good reason for his actions and behaviours. It is up to us, as humans, to appreciate why a horse is behaving as he does and to read the many signals a horse sends out every second. By observing and reading our horses, we can build a superb relationship through understanding their behaviour and adapting our training techniques to suit the horse's needs and way of learning.

Horses in the field
Socializing in groups

Horses are very social animals and love the company of their own kind. If they are denied contact with other horses, especially over a long period of time, many problems can arise, manifesting in mental, physical or behavioural difficulties. The herd is the basis of equine society, providing its members with safety in numbers, the opportunity to reproduce, friendship and support.

Family life

For horses living in the wild, a typical herd would consist of one stallion (male), several mares (females) and their offspring. Domesticated horses rarely live in such natural groups, but by imitating nature as closely as possible we can help our horses live happy, secure lives. This group of six has lived together for several years and includes one mare and her two sons, another mare and two more geldings (neutered males). Occasionally there are minor disputes, as you would expect in any community, but generally there is mutual cooperation. The fact that these horses are all standing close together and are relaxed shows that they all accept each other and are happy to have each member of their group in their individual personal space.

Did I invite you?

Just as humans are comfortable with friends standing close, and are wary of strangers making physical contact, so it is with horses. These two are part of the herd shown opposite and mutual grooming is a pleasurable experience for both. Touch is very important to horses and here it helps to strengthen the bond between them. When a horse trusts and likes his owner he will often offer to groom his human!

Feminist society

The movie portrayal of a stallion leading and protecting his herd is wide of the mark, as equine society is female-dominated. The herd leader is usually a mare: she makes the decisions about moving the herd on to fresh grazing and hands out discipline. Mares are fiercely protective of their offspring and usually produce foals late at night or very early in the morning, giving the foal time to get used to standing and moving undisturbed.

Learn with mother... and aunty

Within the herd, the mares hand out discipline – here the larger foal has overstepped the mark and is promptly told off by another mare. Mares and foals recognize each other's calls, which helps them locate each other. Foals often play together, but have frequent breaks in order to return to their dam and drink from her udder.

Follow me

Horses are very social animals and follow each other's lead. In this case, several new horses have arrived in a field alongside the summer home of this small herd. As soon as the horses are turned back into their field after an evening check, they follow the oldest mare as she heads back to their new-found friends. Following a lead can be turned to our benefit, when persuading horses to go over certain obstacles such as ditches, or into water for instance.

DID YOU KNOW?

❑ Mares tend to give birth to their foals either late at night or early in the morning. Within an hour of being born a foal is up on his feet. In the wild this is essential for survival. However, domesticated horses still follow this pattern.

The bold one

Watch horses at liberty in the field and you will soon start to recognize the different characteristics of each individual. Young horses are especially revealing: this young colt is bold and inquisitive. He is the one who marches up and investigates strangers in his field – there is no hiding behind others for him. This kind of boldness will be useful in the eventing career that is planned for him.

All legs

When foals are born they always look extremely gangly – this is because in the early months of life their legs are about 90 per cent of the length they will reach at maturity. If you watch foals in the field, you will see that they often have to bend their front legs so that they can reach the grass with their noses. However, they soon master their limbs and are ready for action, playing with their friends.

I'm out of here!

Horses have two survival mechanisms – flight or fight. They prefer the first option. Living in a herd means that the majority of the group can eat, drink, sleep or relax while someone else stays on guard. If danger is scented, seen or heard, the guard horse will alert everyone else by his body position and the herd takes off. Horses run first and ask questions later. If a horse is unable to run then he will fight using his teeth, feet and body. Horses are very agile. Watch them in a field – if one is cornered, he will twist and turn in a small space to avoid being kicked by another horse.

Follow the leader

If a horse is worried about something he takes comfort from the alpha (lead) horse in his group. If the horse that is normally the leader walks past a scary object, then the frightened horse will gain confidence and follow her. The dark bay horse on the left is the youngest member of a six-strong herd and has just encountered an unusual hazard in the riding arena. He seeks reassurance from two members of his herd who are grazing alongside the school. The key to being successful with horses is to become their trusted leader, someone who never lets them down and always looks out for them.

Party animals

Horses do not like being on their own. It is in their nature to live and play with other horses. They need the security of equine company – otherwise, how can they relax to eat and sleep, find the courage to deal with intruders in their field, scratch the tricky places they cannot reach easily and so on? Horses depend on each other, so find it difficult to cope with a solitary life.

DID YOU KNOW?

❑ Horses that are pair bonded may suffer separation anxiety when one horse is taken out of the field. Initial mild anxiety may escalate into a serious problem, in which case professional help should be sought.

Don't leave me

This horse is becoming anxious, as his routine has been changed and his friends have still not joined him. If left like this for much longer he would start running up and down the hedge line, calling frantically for them. Horses that are separated from others, especially if they have a special bond, may fret all day.

Special friends

The bond between a mare and foal is very close, but older horses can also form special friendships. The two horses will seek out each other's company and show great attachment to each other, sharing pleasures such as mutual grooming. If two friends are permanently separated, the horses may go through a process which is similar to grieving.

Two's company

Horses often pair up and have a really close relationship with another horse. This is known as pair bonding and often, but not always, happens between horses of roughly the same age, sex and height. These two are older horses who have been close friends for ten years. Fortunately, they have never been separated for long periods of time, but both owners are aware that if long-term separation does occur each horse would need sympathetic help to adjust to their new situation.

DID YOU KNOW?

❑ Horses are very spatially aware – their own personal space measures around 4–5m (13–16ft). Into this space they willingly allow horses and humans they like and trust. In domestic life a horse may often be handled by someone he does not like – in such cases the horse is often anxious or nervous.

My best friend

The chestnut horse would never tolerate this behaviour from anyone other than her pair bond. The pony is resting his head on his friend's buttock so that he can doze and is kept free of flies by her swishing tail. Pair bonds can be spotted as each allows their friend much more access to their personal space – even eating out of the same bowl or sharing the same strand of hay.

This is my space

If a horse is worried by the presence of another horse such as one who has bullied him, or a human who has perhaps abused him, then he will prefer to keep well away from that particular animal or person. In the domestic situation this is often difficult. Care therefore needs to be taken when allocating stables to ensure that neighbours get on – here you can see one horse's aggressive behaviour towards another. Fortunately, in this instance the aggression is having no effect.

I'll say this only once!

The obvious aggression shown by the horse pictured above is missing here. The grey horse is telling the chestnut horse that he is not interested in rising to his playful persistence, and is issuing a clear but muted warning that he wishes to be left alone.

Playing

Horses play throughout their lives, as a means of learning social skills when young, and later to express their general *joie de vivre*. They indulge in play with their own kind and with their owners, but in each case it is important that the horse understands the limits on his behaviour and does not overstep the boundaries. For instance, it is not uncommon for young foals to present their backsides to humans, as they greatly enjoy being scratched at the top of their tails. This can be a great game with a youngster but is not so funny if an big, fully-grown horse does the same.

Play and learn

Play begins at home, with a young foal initially playing with his dam, grabbing hold of her neck, mane, tail, headcollar – in fact, anything that the foal can get his gums, and later his teeth, around. All youngsters explore things with their mouths, and this play will later move on to other objects that will feature in their lives, such as grooming brushes, lorry ramps, saddles, fences, buckets and so on. By using his mouth and feet to explore new areas or objects, the young horse will be able to satisfy himself as to whether a new area is safe or not.

Group games

By playing games with other foals, youngsters learn to develop their proficiency in galloping, turning, stopping, changing pace, leaping into the air, bucking and twisting. All of these attributes are useful to the wild horse who needs to protect himself from predators. Domestic horses do not have such worries, but their basic instincts still prepare them for such a life.

Nature's way

Young horses have natural urges – this young colt indulges in sexual games, grabbing hold of his dam's neck and then trying to mount her. She is not at all concerned by her son's activities and a few minutes later he is pushed up against her flank, his nose seeking out her udder so that he can have a drink.

DID YOU KNOW?

❏ Young horses playing together will move other youngsters out of the way in the same way as their dams have moved them – pushing or nipping another horse on the head or backside, depending on which end they want to move.

All kinds of friends

Horses who have missed out on the socialization period as youngsters need careful integration into equine society. This horse spent the first eight months of his life in and out of the vet's surgery and was restricted to the company of his dam. It has taken some time for him to catch up on his equine social etiquette. As he had lots of human contact as a foal he still enjoys this, often walking up to his owner in the field and presenting his ticklish spots.

Exploring

In the wild, horses roam over large areas of land and their very survival depends upon them remembering where the grazing is good, where there are water supplies and so on. They have an amazing ability to remember how things are in their world and are incredibly suspicious if anything is different to the map they have in their head. In domesticated horses, we can see this instinct come into effect in their reaction when we add new objects into their usual familiar surroundings.

What on earth?

This young horse has been into the arena on many occasions, but this is the first time that plastic has been placed in the middle. His immediate reaction on seeing it is to stop. All his senses are employed as this new object could mean danger to him. Within a split second he has used his flight mechanism of survival and has galloped off. However, he is confined by the arena boundary and cannot put the usual quarter of a mile (400m) between himself and the dangerous object. This is known as the horse's flight distance – after this he will normally stop, turn and weigh up the offending hazard. In this case, the horse cautiously approached the plastic and, with the comforting presence of his owner, was soon walking over it.

DID YOU KNOW?

❏ Handlers and riders often create problems for themselves simply because they do not allow their horses the time they need to check out whatever is worrying them. People often make matters worse by hassling the horse, or by becoming anxious themselves which is immediately transmitted to the concerned horse.

Testing, testing

Walking into a lorry may be an everyday occurrence for some horses, but initially it is a very worrying situation for the horse. Everything in his body says danger: why should an animal that is vulnerable to being preyed upon walk into a confined area from which he has no escape? First, this youngster has to convince himself that the ramp is safe for him to step upon. If a horse injures his feet or legs he is in extreme danger, as he can no longer run away. Therefore, it is usual for horses to paw or stamp on something strange on which they are expected to walk.

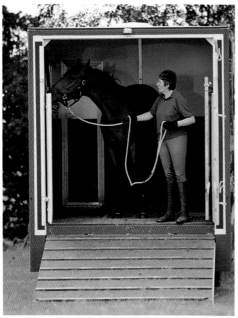

I just need to try this...

Once in the lorry, the young horse wants to reassure himself, so he licks or gets hold of the various surfaces. It is his way of investigating whether this area is safe for him – it is not wilful destruction or bad behaviour on the part of a young horse, but simply a display of his innate survival mechanisms. Once he has satisfied himself that being in the lorry is safe, he will no longer have to use his mouth and feet to explore and test.

Next door neighbours

Horses of all ages, but especially youngsters, are inquisitive. In the wild they have to be in order to survive. This youngster raises his head to peer over bars at the top of his stable's dividing wall, in order to see and smell what is happening next door. In this case, his neighbour was being hot shod so there was a strange smell of burning horn, smoke and the noise of a farrier hammering on a horse's shoes.

DID YOU KNOW?

❑ Most horses will feel more comfortable in a stable with partition bars, rather than a partition wall. The bars enable horses to see and touch each other so that they are not totally isolated. The bars should be close enough together so that a hoof cannot get caught in them.

Super sensors

Watch a horse closely and you will see how much he uses his muzzle to investigate, select and communicate. If left naturally, a horse has extensive whiskers on his nose and lips. These are also present around the eyes, and help to warn the horse of anything near his head. The horse's muzzle has thin skin and is supplied with lots of nerve endings. As the senses of smell and taste are also here, this area is an extremely powerful tool for the horse to use in understanding his environment.

Aaahh, that's the right place!

Rolling allows the horse to scratch himself in places he may otherwise find difficult to reach and it enables him to shed his coat more easily. Rolling also leaves each horse's scent on the ground, and as there is usually a rolling patch, the scents are mixed together to produce a unique herd smell that helps the horses to bond.

A new home

If a horse moves into a new field he will explore the new area, using his senses of sight, sound, touch and hearing. However, before letting your horse loose to explore by himself, it is good practice to lead him around the field boundaries so that he is aware of them before he indulges in a galloping session.

21

Weather

The modern horse's ancestors evolved in several different climatic regions, adapting themselves to the prevailing conditions. Arabs, for example, lived in deserts and so have fine coats to help with heat dissipation. Horses that lived in colder regions have developed coats with a two-layer system which traps air and keeps them warmer.

Wind

Windy conditions often do not bother horses in their own environment as they can adjust their position to suit themselves – this inevitably means hindquarters facing into the wind. However, when ridden they may have to face the wind and walk into it. The horse usually lowers his head and tucks his nose in, much as we bow our heads when walking into wind. It is when wind is accompanied by driving rain that horses look particularly miserable.

Heat

Heat brings its own problems: increased flies, lethargy and the risk of sunburn. Some horses can have very pink muzzles and these are usually prone to sunburn.

Sunscreens have now been developed for equines. Flies are a constant nuisance in hot weather and often cause horses to stamp their feet, shake their heads and swish their tails frantically.

Cooling down

When the weather is hot some horses, like humans, cope with work better than others. Your horse is bound to sweat and, if the weather is really hot, it is important that you help him to cool down by sloshing lots of water over him, removing the excess and then repeating the washing process.

DID YOU KNOW?

❏ When competing in hot, humid conditions, the internal temperature of a horse can be raised considerably. In preparation for the Atlanta Olympics in 1996, much research was carried out to determine the best way of quickly cooling down horses that exerted themselves.

Snow

In countries where snow is part of winter life, equestrian sports continue unabated. However, where the arrival of snow is not such a frequent event, horses are often seen walking rather strangely – this is because the snow balls up under their feet and they have to cope with mini stilts. Greasing the underside of the horse's feet can sometimes help. In the wild, horses have to paw away at the snow to access the vegetation underneath, or paw at ice to reach water. Domestic horses can also be seen doing this.

Reactions to people – being caught

Confinement, or restriction of movement of any kind, is contrary to the horse's nature – after all, he is a creature who is used to running free, moving at will and who equates restriction of any kind to danger. It is a tribute to the generous nature of horses that they allow humans to do so much both to and with them that is contrary to their most basic instincts.

For a horse to allow himself to be caught is a leap of faith and it is important that his owner does not, in the horse's eyes, let the animal down. For instance, catching a horse and then abusing him in some way would naturally make the horse wary of being caught again. This abuse could take the form of something seemingly harmless, such as catching the horse and then keeping him confined for a long period without turning him out each day, but has to be considered from the horse's point of view.

I'm being followed

There is no point in pursuing a horse that is tricky to catch. This only reinforces the idea the horse already has – that you are a predator and are to be avoided. Horses are prey animals and, although they have been domesticated for many years, their innate programming tells them to get away from any perceived danger.

Time to leave!

How you approach a horse you want to catch is important. Marching purposefully towards him carrying a headcollar, immediately alerts this horse to the person's intent. Horses who are known to be difficult to catch need a different approach if you are to succeed.

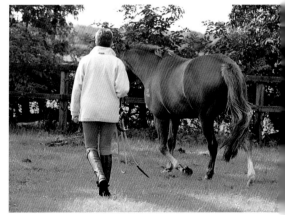

What have you got?

To be successful in catching a horse you need to act less like a predator and more like a prey animal. Prey animals that want to get to a water hole safely are used to making their way gradually towards their objective. They may have to take a few backwards steps if a predator appears, but they resume their journey, taking more forward steps and methodically moving closer to their goal. The same method works with catching horses. The person needs to adopt less aggressive body language than in the picture on page 24 (bottom): note the rounded shoulders, the lack of eye contact with the horse and the quieter, more passive body language. Note also how the horse is interested and inquisitive, as he sees no reason to be worried by the person's presence.

Nice and easy

It is now a simple matter of slipping on the headcollar, but note that the handler does not rush the process nor make sudden moves that would spell danger to the horse and startle him. Horses like to be handled in a quiet, confident mann.r.

DID YOU KNOW?

❏ Your horse will be easier to catch if he is used to you visiting him in the field, offering him a scratch or a rub, and then leaving him alone. If your horse associates you with pleasure rather than just work, he will start to approach you when you enter the field.

Reactions to people – strangers

If a horse's contact with humans has not been enjoyable he is likely to avoid their company, but if horses are used to good relations with people they may well lavish their attention on any passing stranger. So, how do you know whether a horse is human-friendly or not?

Who's this then?

Footpaths often wind their way through fields containing livestock. The arrival of this walker in the field, for example, has aroused the interest of the horses closest to the gate. Although the grey is interested in this new development, his body is generally relaxed and he is happy to stand and observe the newcomer to his field. Very few horses are seriously aggressive towards humans, and those that are have often had a nasty experience at a human's hands. If a horse immediately gallops up to you then care is needed – such horses are obviously bold and unworried by humans. If the horse's ears are back, his head snaking out in front of him and his teeth showing, you should rightly expect trouble and would be wise to leave the field as quickly as possible by the nearest exit.

Got anything for me?

These horses are curious rather than aggressive – you can see how their ears, eyes and bodies have a soft appearance rather than the hardness associated with tension or aggression. They gently nuzzle around the walker's pockets, hoping for food. Do not feed treats as this may cause the horses to argue among themselves, and you may get caught in the crossfire. Instead, use the palm of your hand firmly but gently to push the horse's head away.

You must have something!

There is always at least one horse that is extremely friendly or hopeful of a treat. Keep walking, but be aware of where the horse is and where any other animals are. This walker could try adopting a more aggresive stance to deter the horse.

Hiding any treats anywhere?

Do not tempt fate by walking past horses with your hands in your pockets, as this is an open invitation for the inquisitive to investigate further. Although this horse has her ears slanting back a little she is not aggressive – compare the look on her face with that of the horse pictured (centre) on page 15.

Reactions to people – generally

Horses have such a wide repertoire of expressions that it is sometimes difficult for less experienced people to understand the message that is being conveyed. The overall picture of the horse's head and body needs to be considered, rather than just taking one aspect, such as the ears, into account. Spend time watching horses so you can recognize their many signals.

I mean what I say!

The chestnut horse on the left is not too keen on other horses or people and can easily encourage people to avoid him because of his aggressive behaviour. He is territorial about his own space, so does not like horses or humans near him in his stable – he also exhibits this behaviour in the field. You can see in the first picture how his ears are well back and how his lips and nostrils look tight. It is not very easy to see his eye – compare his eye to the one in the picture of a mare grazing, opposite. What can be seen of this horse's neck also shows tension.

In the second picture you can see how he has thrust his head at the horse and handler, pinned his ears back even further and started to part his lips ready to bite. This horse definitely means business.

DID YOU KNOW?

❏ A horse's aggression may be caused by many different factors including pain, fear, hormones, a violation of his personal space, play and food. In order to deal with the problem, the root cause has to be identified first.

Me? I'm just scratching

Now look at the expression on this horse. His ears are slightly back but they are floppy, showing that he is relaxed and is not contemplating trouble. His eye is also much bigger and softer. Note also how his lips are loose.

I'll just keep an eye on you

Eyes can tell us a great deal about a horse's state of mind. Although she is grazing, this mare is very aware of the photographer and is rather anxious. Her eye is still big and soft but there is a worry line above it. This horse is especially sensitive and becomes very anxious if loud, aggressive people are around.

What's so funny?

Is this horse laughing? Many people would think so, but she's actually performing a posture known as 'flehmen'. Curling back the top lip and raising her head enables her to use her Jacobson's organ more effectively. This organ is found towards the top of the nasal passages and is used to investigate fully a particularly intriguing smell.

29

Reactions to other animals

Predators chase their prey or leap on them without warning, having suddenly appeared from hiding places. Horses, being prey animals, are therefore very wary of any animals that behave like predators.

Some of the animals they meet in everyday domestic life, such as dogs, are indeed predators. For horses to curb their natural prey animal instincts, they need to be introduced carefully to other creatures.

Start young

The best time to introduce any animal to another species is when the animal is young. He is very impressionable at this age and you can make him accept all kinds of experiences. However, you must ensure that experiences are positive.

DID YOU KNOW?

❏ Introductions to other animals should not involve either animal being outnumbered or being deprived of a means of escape. Nor should a frightened animal be forced to mix with another species. For instance, some people mistakenly believe that confining a horse with another animal that frightens him, will teach the horse to accept the other animal. Occasionally this works, but this technique is known as 'flooding' and is a high-risk way of training. The horse may be so scared by the experience that he is never able to overcome his fear of the animal.

Lucky one of us is sensible!

This older horse is being subjected to a terrier rushing towards him, barking madly. Fortunately for the terrier, the horse has been socialized with dogs and shows little interest – the horse's ears register his rather contemptuous acknowledgement of the dog. Even when the terrier runs around him, snapping at his heels, the horse does not show any sign that he is likely to retaliate. This situation could easily arise when the horse is ridden out, so it is useful to habituate your horse to the presence of dogs at an early age.

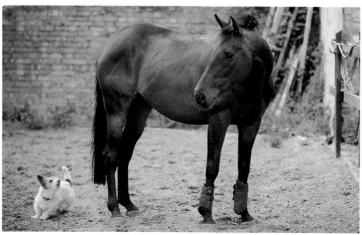

DID YOU KNOW?

❑ When introducing dogs and horses to each other, it is best to keep both animals as immobile as possible and only gradually introduce movement. When a dog is happy about a horse walking around him, and does not try to lunge at the horse, you can lead the horse around him at a trot.

Come on, then!

This horse has probably benefited from some form of socialization period with dogs, as the dog does not overly worry him. However, rather than ignoring the dog as the first horse did, this one is prepared to tell the dog off. Although it is unusual for horses to chase dogs, it does sometimes happen. Remember that horses usually run rather than fight, and it is especially unusual to see a prey animal taking on a predator.

Pigs

Many riders will say that pigs seem to cause their horses great anxiety. This may seem strange, as pigs are not predatory and are so much smaller than horses. The answer probably lies in the depths of each animal's evolutionary past: the horse was once a much smaller animal and could have faced attacks from boars. Domestic horses certainly seem prepared to regard pigs as animals to be avoided. To overcome the problem a horse needs to be habituated to pigs. This process is a gradual one whereby the horse accepts the presence of pigs, having been introduced to them in a variety of contexts: with the pigs in a field, alongside the horse's field; with the pigs in a field alongside the stables and within view of the horses, for example. This is not a process that can be rushed, as the animals have to develop true acceptance of each other. Some breeds of horse also need more time – Arabs and Thoroughbreds can be more reactive than other breeds, for example.

Friends

Chickens are also prey animals and do not really pose a threat to a horse. One way in which a chicken, or any bird, can startle a horse is by getting airborne – often it is the sudden sound and sight that makes the horse start. However, horses that are introduced to chickens at an early stage are soon happy to share fields and stables with them. Other farm animals such as cattle, sheep and goats can initially cause anxiety to horses. However, when the horse realizes that these animals will move away when he approaches, he is usually okay.

Breeding

A mare's pregnancy lasts for approximately 11 months. With domesticated horses, it is usual practice for a mare to keep her foal at foot until the youngster is six months old. The foal is then weaned and lives independently of the mare – many foals no longer have any contact with their dams after this time. In the wild, the foal would stay with its mother until the arrival of the next foal and would not leave her herd until it was two or three years old. A traumatic weaning can have far-reaching effects.

This is tricky!

Even though this foal is several weeks old the process of getting up still looks rather ungainly. Yet within an hour of birth this youngster would have been on his feet. A newborn foal experiments studiously and inevitably collapses in a heap several times before rising triumphantly, albeit still wobbling a little. The persistent attempts are instinctive, as in the wild the foals have to be ready to accompany the rest of the herd at a moment's notice.

DID YOU KNOW?

❑ Behavioural problems with horses may be rooted in a traumatic weaning. Some people still practise the sudden separation of dam and foal, often keeping them in dark stables with the top door shut. Kinder ways do exist!

The milk bar

Foals search out their dam's teats at regular intervals in order to access milk. When the foal is first born he instinctively finds himself looking in the right area for the milk bar, but his dam may have to help him a little. It is not unusual to see mares gently nudging their foals in the right direction. Sometimes a little guidance from a human helping hand is needed. Once the foal knows where to go, however, he is able to home in easily and can be quite demanding.

Mum always loves me

Mares are, on the whole, incredibly patient with their offspring, especially as it is usually the dam who initially bears the brunt of her playful foal's activities. As the youngster grows and becomes more demanding, so she will be less patient and sharper with her admonishments. Foals quickly become quite independent, spending time away from their dam's side, exploring the world around them and playing with other foals.

Anything you can do

Foals will follow their dam's example as they learn about the world. If a mare is trusting and accepting of humans, then the foal is unlikely to have an issue with people (unless something horrible happens to him). If mares are easy to catch and good to load they set a good example to their foal.

Horses in the stable
Grooming

Watch horses in the field and you will often see them grooming each other. This always appears to be an enjoyable activity, so why does your horse pull faces at you when you wield a brush? Why does he refuse to pick up his feet when you ask? As always, the answer lies in the horse's natural instincts.

Damn, she's supposed to be worried now!

This is the horse pictured on page 28. He is very territorial about his space and does not like anyone intruding. Over time he has learnt that acting in this aggressive way has meant that people avoid him, so he has effectively trained people rather than them schooling him. This is not uncommon – although many horses do not have to use such extreme body language in order to keep people away from them. Now this horse is being retrained to accept people in his space – he is learning that his current handler is not frightened by his behaviour and that she will quietly persist until she has finished her work.

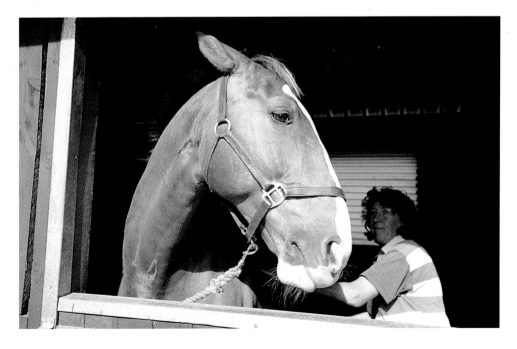

DID YOU KNOW?

❏ It is a good idea to get young horses used to being handled all over their bodies. Run your hand firmly but gently all over their bodies, including their legs. Then you can progress to using a soft brush. To start with, keep the sessions short but frequent.

Take it easy!

There may be other reasons for face pulling – for instance, some horses are extremely sensitive or thin-skinned and do not enjoy the sensation of being brushed. They may pull faces or snap or bite at their handler, or they may grab hold of something else in the stable in order to vent their distress. If your horse acts in this way, investigate the reason for his behaviour and try to eradicate the cause. For instance, thin-skinned horses prefer softer brushes to be used on them, or for mud to be carefully removed by hand or by washing off.

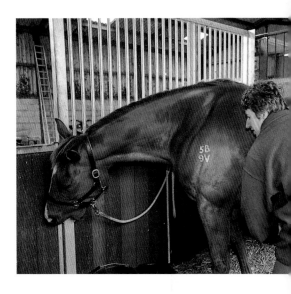

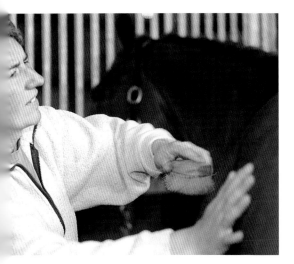

Advance warning

If your horse has a tendency to kick out when grooming, keep one hand on the stifle area. You can then feel him as he moves to kick so you have a little more warning. Some people like to tie a horse up for grooming, whereas others use a headcollar and long rope so that they can still control the horse's head and neck and, therefore, his hindquarters.

I'll just have a little nap

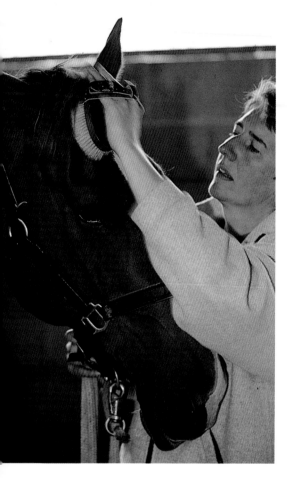

Horses may become sceptical of grooming if they have been hurt in the past. Take care, especially when grooming areas like the head where there are bony projections. Remember to untie the horse when grooming the head so that if he pulls back for any reason (such as sensitivity around the poll) he is not hurt even more. Remember to talk to your horse – this mare will rest her head in the handler's arms and snooze! Spend time grooming young horses as this accustoms them to contact and helps to instil some discipline, for instance, having to be tied up. Keep sessions short initially.

DID YOU KNOW?

❏ Grooming fulfils several purposes. As well as improving appearance it helps to promote health. It removes waste products, stimulates the circulation of blood and lymph. Grooming also helps to improve muscle tone.

❏ A thorough grooming has the most effect when done after exercise as the horse's skin is warm, the pores are open and scurf and dust has risen to the surface. Daily attention to the feet is vital.

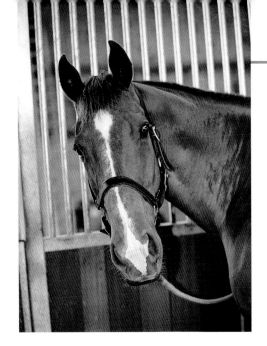

Can I groom you?

Your horse may enjoy the grooming process so much that he offers to groom you – take this as a compliment, but be careful as horses use their teeth rather vigorously when scratching each other! When you groom a horse you have to use your hands all over his body – this includes vulnerable areas such as the belly, neck and legs that are prime targets for predators. It is a sign that your horse trusts you if he lets you handle all areas of his body.

You want WHAT?

Experiencing difficulty when picking up a horse's feet is to be expected. Think about it from the horse's perspective. He needs control of his feet and limbs so that he can flee at will if danger threatens – this really is a matter of life or death to a horse. Through sympathetic training he will hopefully learn that giving his feet to a human for a short while is fine. During this training a horse will inevitably try to put his feet down before the person has finished. If the person hangs on to the foot in the mistaken belief that the horse has to be shown who is boss, then the horse may well be frightened. As a result, he will become mistrustful and even more sensitive about having his feet picked up. You need to build the horse's tolerance of having his feet lifted and handled gradually. To do this, he must never be frightened, but he must know that you will quietly persist until the job is done. Always make it easy for a horse to lift his leg by ensuring that he is first standing in a balanced way.

Tack

Care should be taken when choosing and fitting tack as it can cause great discomfort to a horse if misused and badly fitted. By objecting to his tack the horse is usually telling you of a problem. These objections may include walking away from you, pulling faces, biting or kicking.

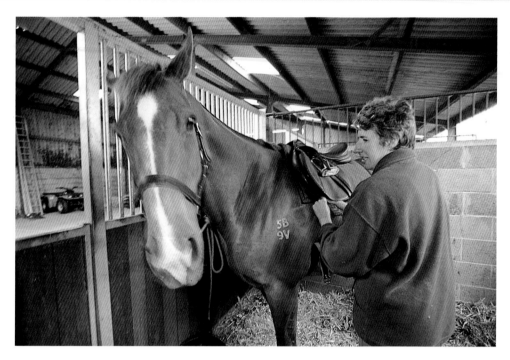

I'm telling you, it hurts!

There is always a reason for a horse's behaviour. You might be told that your horse has always pulled a face when girthed up, but this does not mean you can ignore him. Your horse will have a reason for his behaviour. There may be many, including back pain from the saddle, or as a result of a heavy or unbalanced rider, soft tissue damage from an old injury or sore muscles because the horse is working incorrectly.

DID YOU KNOW?

❏ A common mistake is for people to put a saddle too far forward on a horse, so that the saddle interferes with the movement of the horse's shoulder. Saddles should fit behind the horse's shoulder blades and not on the shoulders.

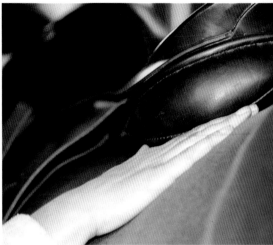

Saddle soreness

Pinpointing the cause of a horse's adverse reaction to tack is an essential first step. If your horse objects to his saddle, check the fit and assess his back for sensitivity. How easily can you slip your hand between the horse and his saddle? It is quite common for saddles to be too tight,

which inhibits the muscle development at the wither, so giving the appearance of hollows on either side. How does the saddle spread the weight? This saddle has good broad panels to dissipate the load, but does not fit well enough to lie evenly on the horse's back. As a result, there will be movement and friction, which could cause discomfort for the horse.

How high can you go?

A horse may try to evade you by raising his head in the air when you try to bridle him. Perhaps he has been banged in the teeth by the bit, or his mouth hurts because he needs dental attention, or he has an issue with his mouth being handled, possibly because someone in the past has hit him.

This is good!

Working a horse's mouth helps to overcome his fear of being touched in this area. The Tellington-Touch Equine Awareness Method (TTEAM) developed by Linda Tellington-Jones involves making small circular movements around the horse's mouth in a specific way. This method begins by working the outside of the face, then the nostrils and the lips, and gradually moves on to the inside of the lips and then rubbing the gums. This helps to build a horse's confidence and overcomes problems brought about by careless bridling or rough handling.

Cuddle those ears

Bridling problems may arise if the horse is wary of having his ears touched, perhaps through rough handling or someone accidentally hurting his ears when removing a bridle. The answer to such problems is to gradually accustom your horse to having his ears touched. Giving the ear a firm stroke from the base to the tip, as recommended by TTEAM (see above) practitioners, is a good way to relax a horse.

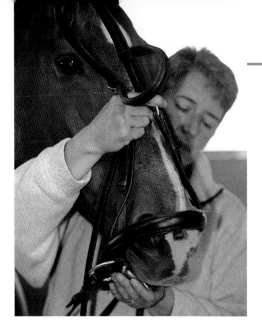

Open wide

Refusing to open the mouth for the bit may be rooted in one of the problems mentioned on page 41. Use your right hand to steady the horse's head and hold the bit in the left hand, perhaps with a little treat such as a piece of apple or carrot, to encourage the horse to mouth and take the bit. Always ensure that your horse's teeth are attended to – this should be done at least twice a year.

DID YOU KNOW?

❏ TTEAM ear touches can be used in an emergency such as colic, as they help to lower a horse's respiratory rate and also affect his digestive system. In such a situation the touches need to be done quickly and firmly.

Not too tight!

Check the fit of your horse's browband – if it is too tight and is pinching his ears he will probably object to being bridled.

Help me relax

Nosebands that are fitted too tightly make it impossible for the horse to relax his jaw and accept the bit. There should be at least two fingers' width between the horse's face and the noseband.

Feeding

Horses living under natural conditions spend around 16 out of every 24 hours eating. If their natural pattern of eating is disturbed, and they eat food that is not naturally their first choice, then digestive disturbances and perhaps changes in behaviour may follow.

Grass, glorious grass

Horses are designed to eat grass. In the wild, they would cover a large distance each day as they grazed. Domesticated horses may have only limited access to grass if they are turned out for just a few hours. In addition, they graze the same paddocks day after day so will not necessarily get the full range of herbage, vitamins and minerals. There may also be a problem, known as laminitis, if a horse has access to large quantities of rich grass. If your horse is wary of walking and tries to take the weight off his front feet by stretching them forward and taking his body weight backwards then urgent veterinary attention is required.

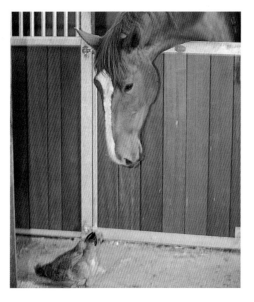

I need to eat!

Horses that are stabled for long periods of time and do not have continual access to hay may develop habits, such as banging on the stable door, windsucking or crib biting. If a horse is unable to eat for most of the day, he will become more food-orientated and more likely to be anxious or aggressive at feed times. In addition, he may resort to chewing his stable door or grabbing hold of it and sucking in air. This is his way of meeting his physiological needs, so stopping the windsucking by fitting a preventative device only adds to the horse's stress levels.

Slow down!

Some horses are greedy and will bolt down their food. Put a large mineral lick into the feed bowl as well so the horse is less able to grab mouthfuls.

DID YOU KNOW?

❏ Horses must be given at least an hour after they have finished a hard feed before they are ridden. This is because when work starts, digestion stops. Horses should be fed little and often in imitation of nature.

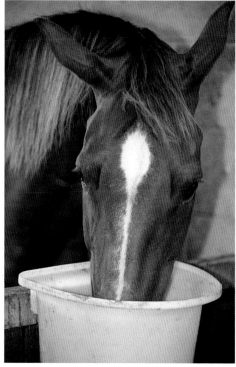

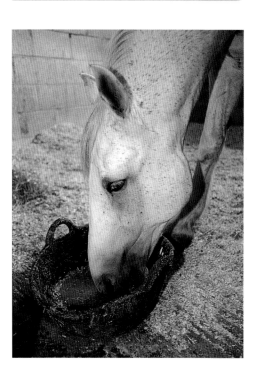

There's something strange in here...

The horse's sense of smell and taste is acute – in the wild, he relies upon the former to give him warning of approaching predators and the latter to help him distinguish nasty and possibly dangerous feedstuffs. It is, therefore, not surprising that horses can detect the inclusion of medicines in their normal feeds. They can often sift out various feedstuffs using their highly mobile lips, a skill which is life-saving in the wild. Many drugs now have flavourings added to make them more palatable to the horse.

45

Sick horses

Horses may not be able to talk, but have many ways of communicating that they are feeling ill. For this reason, owners have to be observant and look out for the physical signs of illness. These can be followed up with checks, such as taking temperature, pulse and respiration.

Look at me

Healthy horses take an active interest in life, whether they are living in stables or out in the field. This field-kept horse receives little grooming so his coat is not shining, but his skin is loose and moves easily – ill horses often have coats that are tight and 'stare'. He moves around the field at all paces, takes an interest in what is happening in neighbouring fields, eats and drinks as expected, and passes droppings and urinates easily and regularly. His owner knows what is normal behaviour for this horse and would immediately investigate if he acted strangely. Even if a horse lives out, it is vital to check him at least twice daily so you are aware of any problems.

DID YOU KNOW?

❑ Caring for a sick horse may mean keeping him in isolation in order to prevent the spread of disease. This needs to be considered when designing a stable yard and is especially important if you decide on a natural system of horsekeeping, such as a communal barn where the horses live together (as opposed to American-style barn stabling).

Writhing around

Horses roll for pleasure and when in pain. Distinguishing the two types is not difficult as in the latter case there is usually sweating, the horse looks distressed and the rolling is much more frequent (the horse may get up and down several times within a short space of time). This sort of behaviour is associated with colic and veterinary advice should be sought.

Hot or cold?

Sweating occurs after a horse has been worked, especially if the weather is hot. This kind of sweating is normal and healthy and is to be expected in the circumstances. When a horse is ill there may be sweating but the horse is not necessarily hot.

Changes and effects

Be aware of everything your horse does – for instance, eating too many apples can cause stomach upsets. Changes in grazing, different feeds, upset routines, excessive stress through travelling, intensive schooling, the loss of an equine or human friend – all can affect a horse's well being.

Look – and see!

Learn to observe your horse. This gelding went down to roll in the field but instead of getting up as usual sat like this, rubbing his tail. He is suffering from sweet itch (a skin complaint), but no one had seen him do this before. Once you have a good idea of what is normal for your horse, you can more easily distinguish anything abnormal. It is helpful to ask yourself questions when observing your horse, such as 'why is he doing that?'

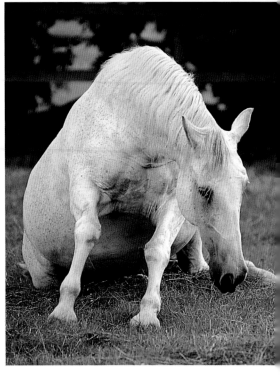

Check the colour

This horse is blowing after exercise, but you can clearly see the salmon-pink membrane in her nostril. This membrane, and those in the eyes and gums, should be salmon-pink if the horse is healthy. Make it part of your daily routine to check signs such as these. You should also know your horse's normal temperature, pulse and respiration rate.

Tell-tale signs

One of the biggest clues that your horse is not well is that he goes off his food and water. On average, a horse will drink about 24–40 litres (6–10 gallons) of water a day and needs to eat 2–2.5 per cent of his bodyweight in order to maintain his weight. The horse's resting pulse is normally 36–42 beats per minute, respiration is 8–15 breaths per minute and temperature is 38°C (101°F).

DID YOU KNOW?

❏ Computer programmes are now available to help you keep records of your horse's veterinary treatment, such as providing reminders of important dates for vaccinations, worming and farriery.

What's different?

Note any changes in your horse's behaviour, as these can be warnings that he is off-colour: he may be lethargic or grumpy, does not want to play, or refuses to jump when he is usually enthusiastic. recognizing the subtle signs means that you can take action sooner and hopefully avoid a minor problem becoming something more serious.

Toys

There are times when a horse's life can become rather boring – if the horse is recuperating from illness and has to be confined to his stable, for instance, or during winter when turn-out time is limited and he inevitably spends more time in his stable out of adverse weather. Equine toys can then help the horse while away the hours.

Let's play ball

A number of toys are available, but most horses seem to prefer the ones that offer rewards! Horse cubes or other concentrate feed can be placed in this toy and will be dispensed if the horse rolls it around enough. Only a small amount of food is dispensed each time. This horse amuses himself with the toy in winter – he is brought into his stable in late afternoon and the ball keeps him occupied until his owner visits in early evening. There are also scented large apple-shaped toys which seem to appeal to some horses.

DID YOU KNOW?

❏ Allowing horses permanent access to hay helps to keep them busy, as they chew 1kg (2lb) of hay up to 6,000 times before swallowing it. The chewing rate for concentrate feeds is much less – about 1,000 chews for 1kg (2lb).

I'm bored!

Not all horses will play with toys. If your horse has to be stabled for long periods, ensure he has hay available at all times as this will keep him occupied and will satisfy his need to chew. You can also provide inexpensive entertainment for him by suspending apples, carrots and swedes on string from the stable roof. Products such as various flavours of horse licks can also be suspended.

Field habits

When there is little grass in a field, horses can also start to look for other ways to keep their mouths and stomachs occupied. Grabbing hold of fence posts and sucking in air is one way, chewing the wood on fencing is another. Once horses have acquired these habits it is difficult to stop their behaviour.

Friends are important

If you can keep your horses as naturally as possible, the chances of problems arising are reduced. Natural horse-keeping includes housing the horses in a communal area rather than individual stables so that they can all interact. If this is impossible, having bars dividing stables, rather than solid walls, allows the horses to see and touch each other.

51

Claustrophobia

You may come across a horse who cannot cope with being confined – rather like some people dread being in small spaces and become extremely agitated and nervous. This can present real problems, especially if you do not have your own facilities at home and have to rely upon livery owners working with you to supply a solution to a horse's problem. If this is the case, look for people interested in natural horsekeeping and horsemanship as they should understand your plight.

What does he really think of his stable?

Take note of how your horse behaves in his stable – it may be that a sudden noisy incident in the yard has unsettled him temporarily, but if he regularly makes a habit of walking around his box, there is probably a more serious underlying issue. Is your horse happy and settled in his stable? Are there any obvious reasons for his behaviour? If he has not been turned out for the winter, for example, you should expect him to be wound up and fed up!

Your horse could be miserable because he is stabled next to a bully, or because he prefers quiet and is in the box which gets more passing traffic than any other!

Another reason could be that he finds confinement stressful. Horses and ponies who are like this may actually try to get out of the box, either by barging through as the door is opened, or by scrabbling over the top door. In such cases, if you give the horses the option of being out, you will find that they usually prefer it, irrespective of the weather. Accommodating such horses need not be that difficult if you have your own facilities and can turn them out all year or keep them in an open crew yard in winter.

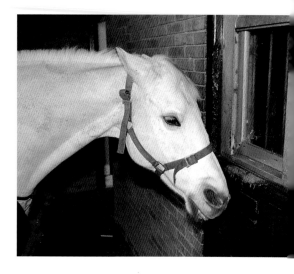

DID YOU KNOW?

❑ There are no quick-fix solutions to equine problems, especially if the cause is deep rooted. Sometimes, people can paper over the cracks and appear to have effected a miracle cure, but the original difficulty soon returns.

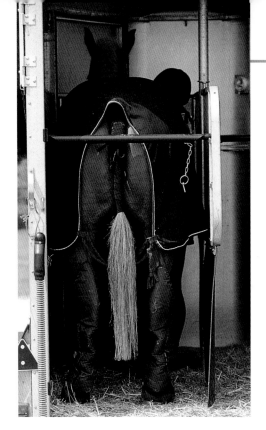

Let me out!

If your horse is troubled by confinement in a stable, he will have even more difficulty with a trailer – so the sensible course of action is to avoid making matters worse. If you have to travel, you need to consult an equine behaviourist well in advance of the journey to see if your horse's problem can be resolved. A horse who has suffered an accident in a trailer may well be fearful of loading again.

The outdoor type

Horses of all types and ages can live out at grass all year round. After all, that is what they do in the wild – and without the luxury of rugs! Horses who become stressed by confinement are happier outside, but they still need the company of other horses. It is important to pay them regular visits and to keep an eye on their general condition and health. Horses who live outside permanently need some form of shelter – either a natural form, such as hedging, or a man-made one.

Riding
Carrying a rider

Despite the fact that they are not particularly well designed for carrying loads, horses have been ridden for thousands of years. Horses have to be educated to accept a rider and if this process is not done thoroughly, the cracks will appear later on. Many riders also forget that horses are very sensitive – they can feel a fly landing on their skin so imagine how it must feel to have a person sitting on their back! Well-balanced riders make life easier for horses.

Please stand still!

Some riders are used to having to get on their horses quickly, as their animals start to move as soon as the rider's foot touches the stirrup. This may occur because the horse has been allowed to do this and does not know any better. Sometimes this has been part of the horse's training (for example, with racehorses), in other cases the horse is genuinely worried and in some instances the horse is simply taking advantage. From a rider's viewpoint, a horse that will not stand still to be mounted is a potential safety risk. The answer lies in retraining the horse, not in getting on quicker. This means that you have to show him that there is no benefit in moving and that, in doing so, it only wastes his own energy.

Feel that saddle!

The process whereby a horse is taught to accept a rider is known as 'starting' or 'breaking in'. If, during this time, the horse does not have the opportunity to fully accept being saddled, he is likely to experiment further with a rider. This usually takes the form of bucking. It is, therefore, vital that a young horse is given the chance to get the feel of a saddle on his back, at all paces.

DID YOU KNOW?

❑ For a horse to work properly and to carry a rider easily, his saddle must fit. A badly fitting saddle hurts the horse and can have a detrimental effect upon his muscle development, movement and temperament.

Setting the pace

The thrill of speed appeals to many riders – but if things get out of hand fun can turn to terror. Very few riders have experienced a genuinely bolting horse: in such cases the horse is in a blind panic and will not see or stop for anything in his path. Most riders, however, have experienced a momentary loss of control when the horse is in charge and sets the pace. If a horse makes a habit of running away the reasons could include: pain caused by the saddle, mouth or teeth; back problems, or pain inflicted by the rider; a tug of war created by the rider pulling on the horse; or a rider who lacks confidence and clings on, frightening the horse.

Traffic and bridleways

Riding out and soaking up the sights and sounds of the countryside is very relaxing. However, this is not the case if your horse is a nervous type, jumping out of his skin every time a bird or rabbit moves. Before venturing out onto public highways your horse needs to have had a good level of training, to have been exposed to many different sights and sounds and to have confidence both in himself and his rider.

Hidden horrors

Hedges hold all kinds of scary monsters if you have a nervous horse – birds and other animals may emerge or there may be a walker tucked away. Many non-horsey people are worried by the sheer size of horses and if they meet one at close quarters they tend to hide away, but this causes a nervous horse even greater concern and creates potential difficulties for the rider. Wherever you ride you must be alert to possible problems, but you have to keep your own nerves under control, otherwise your horse will sense your anxiety and react to it.

Anything can happen

Being prepared for the unexpected is a good maxim for all riders – your horse may well be used to traffic, but the sudden emergence of a barking dog, or children shouting through the window, can upset even a quiet horse.

DID YOU KNOW?

❑ Boost your horse's confidence by riding out with another horse that is calm and well behaved in traffic. This will also make you feel happier and more relaxed – and this in turn will be felt by your horse.

Eagle eyes

Horses are very quick to notice any changes in their surroundings – you can see how the presence of something unexpected has caused this horse to move out towards the centre of the road. There is potential here for a bigger problem to develop. If your feel your horse may react to a roadside hazard, turn his head and body away from the object so that he is travelling down the road at a slight angle.

Towing terrors

Vehicles approaching from behind, especially if towing noisy trailers, will cause a horse to startle. Although the horse has virtually 360-degree vision he does have two blind spots – immediately in front and immediately behind him. To the horse it can seem as though something has suddenly appeared in his field of vision. Large obstacles are even more threatening, especially if they are noisy as well. The horse that is normally quiet and sensible will often just need some time to work out what is happening.

DID YOU KNOW?

❏ Some national horse associations offer training or tests and it is a good idea to take advantage of these. Road-related training could help you gain better control of your horse, as well as a better understanding of why he reacts as he does when out on roads or trails.

Leading the way

If a horse is genuinely frightened of something on the road he may well try to spin round, move backwards at a great rate and generally resist all attempts to make him go past the object. Using force to make him go forward will not help and will only make matters worse. When a horse is scared, he needs to take reassurance and a lead from someone he can trust. In the wild he would turn to the alpha horse – this is a role the rider has to adopt. This may involve getting off and leading the horse past the hazard.

Off-road fun

Some farmers and landowners are making their facilities available to horse riders in return for annual or daily fees. These off-road riding routes may also include optional jumps. As roads become increasingly busy so entrepreneurs will recognize the need for more off-road riding and start to provide it. Some riders take a proactive approach and present the idea to landowners. Such paid-for routes are a useful option, especially if an area has only limited public riding access.

Response to the rider

Horses are very perceptive creatures. They are adept at understanding non-vocal clues and read a person's body language all the time. They know whether someone is competent, worried, upset or angry. You cannot hide your feelings or your mood from a horse!

The price of tension

These two pictures show the effects of a horse sensing and reacting to the rider's feelings. If a rider feels insecure, the thought that goes through their brain translates into an action. In the first picture, you can see how the rider has tensed up, curled her upper body and grabbed hold of the horse's mouth via the reins. Her legs are also tense against the horse's flanks. As a result the horse looks worried, has tensed up and quickened his pace. The combination of a nervous rider and a nervous horse promotes an increasing spiral of anxiety, leading to fear and even terror.

Why should this be? To the horse, the rider feels very much like a predator on his back – the horse can feel the sensations of the weight on his back clinging on and digging in claws (the rider's heels and hands). As a prey animal, the horse is programmed to rid itself of such unwanted attention. If this horse were not so well trained, it might have bucked, reared and plunged by now. Even though the horse is well trained, you can see how the rider's fearful thoughts and actions have affected him.

Now look at the second picture and see how the rider has relaxed. This is immediately communicated to the horse, who also relaxes in response.

Ask for help

If you are having problems with your horse try to find an experienced, sympathetic instructor who has the knowledge and understanding to read both your horse and you! The way in which your instructor communicates with you will have a tremendous impact upon your progress, especially if you are a nervous or novice rider. A good teacher will help you to understand your horse better and teach you how to master your thoughts and actions so that the responses you get from your horse are the ones you want. It is not always easy to find the right instructor. Have lessons with several if necessary, in order to find the one that suits your needs. The way in which an instructor communicates with you and the words or images he or she uses, can greatly affect your understanding of his or her explanations.

DID YOU KNOW?

❑ Riders can learn to control their nerves through a variety of techniques. Neuro-linguistic programming (NLP) seems to offer an effective solution and is becoming increasingly popular in riding circles.

Response to other animals

A horse's natural reactions are part of his make-up and so whether he is being ridden, handled from the ground or is at liberty, his reactions will show themselves. Through a process known as habituation, a horse can be gradually accustomed to dealing with many of life's challenges – including other people, other horses, other animals and the environment – as he learns to ignore what is not a threat to his survival.

A friend ahead

Whether your horse is used to being ridden out alone or in company, you can guarantee that if he spots a strange horse ahead he will certainly be interested in catching up. This interest may manifest itself as an increased spring in his step and a slightly longer stride, or an outright decision to take charge and reach the strange horse, ignoring the rider's requests to slow down. The latter situation is potentially very dangerous and indicates both a horse with insufficient schooling and exposure to the world and a rider who has over-horsed herself.

It is natural for horses to be curious about other horses and to want to be with their own kind. For this reason, they are suited to activities that involve being in a group, such as sponsored rides, racing or hunting.

However, we also require our horses to leave the herd and compete on their own. When horses are not too keen on this idea they show their feelings by refusing to leave their friends in the collecting ring and enter the jumping ring. If told off by their rider, they may object more strongly and buck, plunge or rear. Often this behaviour is disobedience and stubborness. In some cases it may be, but

often it is a result of the horse having had insufficient schooling to cope with these situations. The answer lies in going back to basics and re-educating the horse. Ask for help if you are unsure how to tackle the problem.

Predator and prey animals can get on

In the wild, dogs are predators and horses are prey animals. As a result, a horse will follow its instincts and run if a dog suddenly rushes from a driveway and barks madly. This behaviour can be altered if horses and dogs are habituated to each other in a safe environment where neither animal feels threatened.

Be aware!

Horses have survived by being very aware of what is happening around them – so strange noises or sudden movements are met by the instinctive reaction of flight. This is why riding out can be fraught with incident – children may be playing in gardens, game birds may take off from verges, litter may be flapping in the hedge and so on. This problem is compounded if the rider is nervous and jumps with fright as well. This will soon be transmitted to even the steadiest of horses, so the rider should learn sports psychology techniques in order to control nerves.

Move 'em out!

Farm animals such as cattle and sheep are prone to making sudden movements and this startles horses. To accustom your horse to farm animals, seek help from a local farmer and introduce your horse to just one sheep, cow or goat at a time. If you flood the horse by putting him in a field full of, say, cattle straight away you can do more harm than good.

Noise

Part of a horse's education should be to accustom him to whatever he is going to meet in our world. By systematically desensitizing our horses to many new experiences we give them a good start and hopefully can avoid placing them in over-stressful situations.

DID YOU KNOW?

❑ Clipping a horse can be a problem because of the noise and vibration of the clippers. By gradually exposing the horse to the noise and feel of the clippers, the horse can progressively understand and accept this situation. This process may take a few days to complete, depending upon the horse's experiences of clipping in the past.

Watch those ears!

Horses have acute hearing – they often hear noises way before the rider does. The rider can 'read' the horse by watching his ears. Both ears forward mean the animal's attention is forward, both back can indicate aggression or pain, or that the horse is listening to something behind or paying attention to the rider. When a horse has divided his attention one ear will point one in each direction. Totally relaxed horses often have their ears flopping sideways.

Running from danger

The natural reaction when a horse perceives danger is to run – so if a grazing horse hears an unexpected noise he will do just as his ancestors did.

Quiet please

The equine occupant of this stable has two hazards to deal with – the noise of the barking dog and the rattling of the door as the dog jumps against it. Not surprisingly, each time the horse reacts by promptly withdrawing into the stable.

A lead

Horses and humans have co-existed for thousands of years, with both species benefiting from the arrangement. Some relationships, such as that between a working cowboy and his horse, are reliant upon the two working together with as little hassle as possible. When a working man relies upon his horse for transport he cannot afford to have silly arguments over crossing a stream or a wooden bridge. He and his horse have to work out a way to get along and get their jobs done.

You must be joking!

A ditch on a cross country course has stopped this horse in her tracks. She is suspicious of this hole in the ground – her instincts are very close to the surface and are telling her to beware. Trying to force the issue only serves to make her more wary; to understand this, adopt the horse's mindset for a while. If this hole in the ground is safe, why has her rider become agitated, giving her no time to think and trying to make her go forward? Surely if there was nothing to worry about, the rider would be calm? If a horse is frightened and a rider tries to make him obey her, the end result is usually a spiralling state of anxiety and temper.

Just follow me

A frightened horse needs to be convinced that there is nothing to worry about. If there were other horses around who could jump the ditch they could provide a lead. If no one is about the rider can provide a lead by getting off and leading the horse across.

Let me think about this

Give horses time to assess the situation they are faced with as they often need to work out what they have to do. Safety is vital so you have to be aware of your position, your horse's position and the possibility that the horse will jump towards you for security.

DID YOU KNOW?

❏ There is a fine line between accustoming an animal to something and pushing them over the edge so that they are more frightened of the initial problem. It is essential to read your horse's reactions every second.

One more time

Build your horse's confidence by repeating the exercise. Do whatever your horse can manage at the time – for instance, it would have been beneficial to have remounted and jumped this horse over the ditch, but on this occasion this was all she could manage.

Training
Schooling

Horses mirror their riders, so if a rider is stiff so is the horse. If a rider lacks confidence, the horse will too. Sadly, it is difficult for many riders to admit that the problems they experience with their horse are of their own making. Horses that lack consistent and progressive schooling will become stiff and will 'motorbike' around corners, find it hard to turn smoothly and so on. To deal with a horse's problem the rider usually needs to look to herself.

First things first

Before any athlete starts serious work they go through a warm-up routine to make sure their muscles are ready. The horse is no exception – and neither is the rider. Start on a fairly loose rein so that your horse can stretch and relax. Take the time to check through your own riding position and remind yourself of its influence upon the horse's movement.

Vary your work

The type of work your horse does will vary according to his level of training, but he must always go forwards willingly. If in any trouble, send the horse forward.
Be considerate when the weather is extreme, either too hot (the horse may be very lethargic) or very cold (the horse may be feeling the cold and will not want to walk endlessly).

Equality rules

If your horse finds it difficult to turn – and it is usually to the right as we mostly handle our horses from the left side – then you need to work on exercises to help him become more supple. You should also check his muscle development as it possible that the horse has a long-term problem due to uneven musculature.

A shake of the head

Throwing the head up and down like this is a clue – this behaviour is typical of horses that are headshakers. It might be an annoying habit to the rider but is considerably more irritating to the horse! It may be allergy related and may possibly be allieviated through complementary therapies. One point of certainty – the horse is definitely not doing this to annoy you or anyone else!

Competitions

Taking your horse to a competition should be fun for both parties. It is a chance for the rider to test their riding and training as well as to have fun. For the horse it is a big change in routine, perhaps involving the stressful processes of loading and travelling. There are new sights and sounds to be experienced, new horses to meet and the horse is expected to perform as well as he does at home! Some horses love going out and rise to the occasion, others become stressed for many different reasons.

Why is this happening?

A horse's lack of performance in the ring may be due to a variety of factors: he could be poorly prepared for the job in hand; be feeling pain or discomfort, if the ground is hard or his saddle does not fit, for example; or he may be hampered by a nervous or badly balanced rider. If a young horse is competing for the first time, he may simply be distracted by all the activity of a show ground. As a general rule for jumping classes, for your own confidence and for that of your horse, it is better to be jumping higher at home than you are in competitions.

Is this the right job for the horse?

The pressure of competitions can affect both horse and rider. Competing is particularly hard for the horse if he is being asked to do something which is beyond his level of training or ability, or he simply does not enjoy the job. Like us, horses have to enjoy what they are doing in order to give of their best. If they are unwilling participants in dressage or jumping, it could be that both they and the rider would be happier if an alternative job was found for them.

This is fun

Sports such as endurance riding are growing in popularity and they pose tremendous challenges to both horse and rider. Long distances need to be covered within certain time limits over a huge variety of terrain. Riders have to know a great deal about getting their horses fit and feeding them, and building a superb bond with them. This is a sport which offers various levels and can be enjoyed by all horses and riders – with the lower levels of pleasure rides involving horses doing what they would do naturally – cross terrain as a group.

Sport for all

Sometimes competitions can become too serious – and although the relatively new sport of 'Trec' has an international level, it also has a growing band of people who enjoy the lower levels. There are a variety of tasks to be performed, from orienteering on horseback, to negotiating small hazards. The competition offers fun challenges to horses and riders – some sections offer alternative tasks – enabling both horse and rider to make the best of their particular talents.

DID YOU KNOW?

❏ Complementary therapies such as aromatherapy, Bach Flower Remedies and homoeopathy can help if a horse or rider is stressed by competition or other difficult situations, such as during firework displays.

Concentration

Ask anyone to recall their best learning experience and the chances are that it will have been fun as well as educational, and challenging but not daunting. It is likely to have been of sufficient duration to enable them to absorb information but not so long as to have been boring. Apply this to teaching your horse and you'll find that progress will be much quicker.

Move slowly... and think!

Before a horse is backed for riding there are exercises that can be used to stimulate his brain and body. Arranging poles in this way to form a labyrinth is one such exercise. The principle is that the horse negotiates turns slowly, so that he is aware of his body movement. Nothing is learned in a rush and the horse is stopped and backed up within the poles to assist with his balance and self-control. When horses have to think about exercises such as these, they tend to lower their heads, have soft eyes and relaxed ears.

Take the time your horse needs

You can improve your horse's flexibility and his ability to judge height and distance by stepping him over raised poles. Start off small and build up – this big horse has to make a deliberate effort to pick up each foot and then choose where to put his foot down. This exercise helps his body awareness and coordination and builds his confidence. You can see the softness in his ears, eyes and face, showing that he is concentrating on his work but is not anxious about the task. Do not hassle your horse during these exercises – he will often need the time to work out the next move.

I'm working it out

This is typical body language for a horse when he is really concentrating and working something out. Once your horse is used to walking on plastic, add water to help prepare him for going into streams.

You could also have him walking between and under sheets of plastic. All this is good preparation for hacking out, travelling in a trailer, having a rider on his back and meeting the unexpected such as rustling bags in hedgerows, umbrellas, flapping laundry and so on.

Thinking is tiring

Having to think and work out problems rather than just running away from them is tiring. This is particularly true for young horses who are not yet used to regular work of any kind. Be aware that mental tiredness may hit a youngster before physical tiredness. Watch out for the signs, such as lack of attention and yawning. Always end a lesson on a positive note and while the horse has enough energy and brain power to absorb the information.

Encouragement

If someone helps you overcome a problem or offers timely, relevant advice, you normally regard such a person with affection and gratitude. The scale of your gratitude may depend upon your perception of the initial problem and the resulting solution. However, there is usually a 'warm' feeling experienced by both the giver and receiver of the advice.

Horses like to be helped too – they face all kinds of obstacles as they live in our world and appreciate assistance and encouragement from their riders or handlers. This encouragement can take many forms.

Be prepared for the unexpected

Let your horse experience new sights and sounds by putting items such as flapping bags, umbrellas, traffic cones and other objects in his environment. This bag in the field resulted in the horses snorting and then backing off, but within a few seconds each horse had approached the bag, sniffed it and then proceeded to ignore it.

If you watch horses in these circumstances you can understand more about their natures by how bold or timid they are, whether they stop and think or stop and then run.

DID YOU KNOW?

❑ Horses are very tactile – stroking or rubbing a horse gives him reassurance.

From ground to saddle

Once your horse has developed the skill of stopping and thinking rather than acting upon instinct, he will be able to use this attribute when ridden. Faced with a large plastic water tray, this horse slams on the brakes. She is allowed the time to check out the 'monster', which is not too frightening after all. On the next attempt she jumps, although you can see that she is giving the 'monster' plenty of room and is still wary (look at the horse's eyes, which are focused on the jump below).

'Thank you' goes a long way

This applies in both the human and horse worlds. Do be aware that as horses are sensitive they appreciate a stroke or a rub rather than a hearty slap. As soon as foals are born their dams clean them, using their tongues. This is the firm, loving touch that a horse is used to, so to really thank and encourage a horse why not imitate this natural feeling?

Fear and nerves

There are degrees of nervousness, ranging from mild anxiety to full-blown fear. Just as some people can appear calm yet are trembling inside, so it is with horses. Some, like the mare featured on pages 84–5, make their feelings and insecurities well known. Others hide their emotions more, and continue to perform until one day something tips them over the edge and they flatly refuse to continue jumping, racing or whatever. Usually these horses have been sending out messages of discomfort or unease for some time, but they have not been recognized as such by people. Riders should always consider the reasons for a change in a horse's behaviour.

What's that?

This horse has seen something in the distance that has aroused his attention. He needs to ascertain whether there is a threat or not. See how he uses his senses: his ears are pricked forward to pick up sounds, his eyes are focused on the distant object and his nostrils are wide, taking in the smells.

Inborn suspicion

Horses have survived thanks to their awareness of the world around them, and these natural instincts can be seen in domestic horses in many instances. This horse is wary of going into the water jump – she has no way of knowing how deep it is, whether a predator is waiting for her, or whether the footing is sound or not. She would much prefer to find another way around rather than face the problem.

Life in a human's world

The difficulty is that the horse now lives in our world and needs to know how to cope with everything we throw at her – being ridden, going into trailers, being jumped, meeting traffic and so on. This horse has had training at home and now needs to put her preparation into practice in the real world. The rider keeps the horse's attention on the task but without forcing the issue. If the horse steps to the side, the rider calmly moves her back on line and praises her when she makes an effort. These efforts may only be small, but in rewarding each try, the handler reassures the horse and builds her trust and confidence. Within a couple of minutes the horse has stepped into the water.

DID YOU KNOW?

❏ Horses are often wary of plastic bags or paper on the roadside because they rustle. To a horse, this may sound like a predator hiding in the hedge or bushes.

What a feeling

Now that the horse has been brave enough to go into the water, she needs time to get used to the experience. This helps to reinforce the lesson the horse has just learnt – that she has no reason to fear going into water. Think of yourself learning a new skill: you need time to assimilate new knowledge and so does the horse.

Too worried to learn

This is the same horse as on page 77. You can see how, by the rider adopting a different, more forceful approach, the horse reacts by becoming tense and ready to fight back. It is very easy for this situation to continue spiralling until both horse and rider have lost control. In this frame of mind, it is impossible for the horse to learn anything useful. This demonstrates the value of staying calm and giving the horse time to work out a solution for herself.

A fantastic capacity...

A horse's natural instincts would tell her to get away from the sight and smell of burning, yet this horse stands quietly while smoke billows around her. Being shod is part of life for domesticated horses and providing they have been schooled sympathetically, horses can be taught to accept this and many other events without distress. This illustrates horses' amazing capacity to put their instinctive behaviour to one side and to learn and adjust to living with humans.

The value of patience

Although this youngster was initially anxious about walking up to this plastic, he has been given the time to approach and explore it in his own way. This involved pawing, stamping and investigating it with his mouth and took several minutes, but the handler's patience has been rewarded as the horse has himself decided that the plastic is nothing to worry about. This problem-solving skill will be useful later as the horse meets new challenges such as ditches on cross country courses.

DID YOU KNOW?

❑ If you are schooling your horse, whether under saddle or from the ground, he must first be relaxed, otherwise his ability to learn is greatly reduced.

Whatever we meet

Calmness is an attribute that is useful to both horses and riders. As they are such sensitive and perceptive creatures, horses soon realize when their rider (and supposed leader) is worried. This, in turn, makes them anxious. So, learning to control their emotions is an important skill for all riders. Once you can do this, you can meet anything with a quiet confidence that instils trust and belief in both your horse and yourself.

Pain

All horses have different pain thresholds. Some animals will compete, and even win, despite the fact that their saddle pinches and their back is sore. Other animals will start to object violently if they feel the slightest discomfort. Good owners will constantly be on the lookout for anything that could adversely affect their horse's performance and will deal with any problems that arise immediately.

Get off my back...

Although horses do buck when playing, there is a difference between the genuine *joie de vivre* buck and the one which means 'get off me'. If a horse's starting has been rushed, he may not have learnt to truly accept a saddle or rider. Another reason for bucking is because the horse is in discomfort or pain – perhaps because of an injury which causes discomfort every time he is ridden.

I don't think so!

Not all horses share the same enthusiasm for jumping, but if a horse that has always been a good jumper starts to refuse there has to be a reason. Pain may well be the problem – if a horse's back, feet or joints hurt when he jumps then he will soon start to avoid the thing that causes the problem. A rider can also cause a horse pain to a horse by pulling him in the mouth when jumping, by banging on the horse's back and by restricting his freedom over the fence. Horses may also start to refuse because their rider is worried about jumping, as this anxiety is transmitted to the horse.

I don't want to!

Common reasons for a horse's reluctance to go forward are examined elsewhere (see pages 58–9, 66 and 84). If a horse is normally forward-going and enthusiastic about his work but gradually becomes less keen, it is worth investigating to see if pain is the issue. The help of your vet, farrier, instructor and therapist can be sought to establish the source of the horse's discomfort.

DID YOU KNOW?

❏ Complementary therapists can often help equine ailments, but before letting anyone loose on your horse, you need to find out more about their qualifications and training. They should also have permission from your vet to treat the horse.

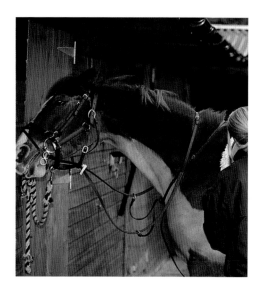

Early warnings!

Whenever you work around a horse, be alert to his reactions and behaviour. Signs of discomfort may be expressed as a slight shortening in his stride, a reluctance to move downhill, face pulling whenever a saddle is brought near, dipping his back when mounted, and in many other subtle ways. If your horse does something out of the ordinary, just ask yourself 'what has happened to cause that reaction?'. Once you know the answer, you will be able to help your horse.

Flatwork

Schooling (that is, on the flat not over fences) should be a regular part of a horse's work. Although often carried out in an enclosed area, schooling can also be done when the horse is being ridden out. Schooling is essential for the developement of a horse's obedience, suppleness, coordination, self-carriage, fitness and general all-round education.

Harness the talent

If you take the time to watch horses at liberty you will see that they can do all the movements required in a dressage test – and more – very easily. They can stop and turn in the time it takes a person to blink, go from walk to gallop smoothly, canter slowly, canter quickly and so on. Good riding and training will ensure that the horse's talent is channelled, but he still retains this natural ability and expression.

Relaxation is key

If a horse is to give of his best he has to be comfortable. Therefore it is important that before you ride you ensure that the horse's tack fits properly (see pages 40–1). As the girth has to be reasonably snug to prevent the saddle slipping, it is good practice to get into the habit of gently pulling the horse's front legs forward after the girth has been tightened. This helps to smooth out any skin wrinkles, which could otherwise cause discomfort.

Horses mirror their riders

Horses are very sensitive to every movement a rider makes and will mirror their rider's good and bad points. If a rider looks down and fails to carry herself properly, the horse's carriage will reflect this. A useful trick is to think of a rider you admire and ride as if you were them as this will have a positive effect on your own confidence and self-image.

Have a plan

Every time you school your horse you need to have a specific objective. This could be achieving fluent transitions from walk to trot or teaching your horse shoulder-in. Your goal needs to be realistic according to your horse's training to date. You can then plan exercises which work towards your objective. Failing to plan your schooling session usually results in frustration, wasted time and a bored horse.

Rewards work wonders

Horses are genuine creatures who, on the whole, like to please their riders, so remember to reward the effort your horse makes. These rewards can take many forms – from an appreciative rub on the neck, to words of praise, to relaxing breaks in the schooling session, to giving the horse his freedom at the end of work to roll and relax.

83

Jumping

Jumping problems may arise for many reasons. These include lack of confidence on the part of the rider or horse – this problem is usually rooted in insufficient or poor preparation and training. A misunderstanding over responsibilities can also cause difficulties: it is the rider's task to get the horse to the fence in the best possible position to jump, but it is the horse's job to jump! Pain or discomfort can also cause difficulties.

I'm not sure about this

Horses differ in character and temperament just as humans do. This mare is very aware of anything out of the ordinary and also has not jumped for a very long time. When faced with a small step down she immediately swings away – reacting instinctively by moving away from something she is unsure about.

Maybe I'll have a look

Without reprimanding her or getting cross, the rider quietly adjusts the mare's position so she is facing up to the problem. The rider allows the mare freedom of rein so the horse can stretch down and work out what she needs to do. Note that there is no forcing of the horse – if she makes a conscious decision to go down the step she will stick to her decision in future and jumping steps should not be a problem.

DID YOU KNOW?

❏ A horse can learn something new from a single experience. The onus is therefore on the trainer to make any experience a positive one for the horse, or he could create problems for the future.

This is OK, I'll go

Within a matter of seconds the horse has worked out that all is well and decides to negotiate the step. She is given the freedom to do so and is then praised for her decision.

Easy!

A few minutes later the mare is happily tackling more than one step. She has accepted her part of the bargain – to take responsibility for jumping – and this has been achieved without coercion.

DID YOU KNOW?

❑ If you are aware of your horse's behaviour and reactions, you can pick up the subtle signals that show something is amiss. Dealing with an issue at the earliest possible opportunity makes life easier for both the horse and rider.

Jumping is fun

Horses and riders can soon lose confidence when jumping. To help to build confidence, tackle small fences often so that jumping is not such a big deal. This fallen tree has become a small, inviting jump. If you jump small obstacles when out hacking, always check the takeoff and landing before jumping and never jump when you are alone.

Shades of light...and darkness

Jumping from light to dark or vice versa can catch out both horses and riders. Both need time to re-focus, especially the horse as he has the responsibility of jumping the fence! Therefore, do not be in too much of a hurry when approaching these fences. Ensure you have enough impulsion and that you give the horse time to assess the situation.

Work over smaller fences initially in order to build confidence and trust in each other. It is very easy to present something badly and cause a horse to fear the experience from that point on – so think before acting and ensure that you set your horse up for success.

Remember that your horse will always act like a horse so do not punish him if he fails to do what you ask. Instead, think about what you are doing and how you can improve things to make communication clearer and give your horse the chance to do the right thing.

Travelling
Loading and unloading

In the horse's eyes, being loaded into a trailer or horsebox and then transported is a life-threatening situation. It is the most unnatural act in the world for him to walk into a dark, confined space, have his means of escape cut off and then be subjected to motion. If the driver is inconsiderate the journey could be awful. Yet many horses do travel countless miles – so what happens to change their way of thinking?

I'd like to think about this

Even though this horsebox has been made as light, airy and attractive as possible, this horse recognizes that going in to it is dangerous. The horse will be using all his senses to register the danger ahead. There are strange smells and he cannot see, hear or smell any of his equine friends.

Horses are generous creatures and do their best to please. The handler firmly but kindly insists that the horse focus his attention on the task ahead – going into the horsebox. The horse makes an effort and lowers his head to sniff the ramp. Before he steps on to the ramp the horse must be convinced that nothing will happen to his feet – if a horse's feet are injured his means of escape and survival is severely compromised. Sometimes horses will paw the ramp too to test it out (in the same way as they would test unknown ground in the wild).

DID YOU KNOW?

❏ Doing less is an under-used approach when it comes to dealing with horses. Keep out of their way and let them assess a situation, but make it easy for them to do what you want.

I appreciate your support

As he has been given the time to check things out and has not been forced or chivvied into making a decision, the horse makes up his own mind to advance a little further into the horsebox. He is rewarded with praise. Nothing horrendous has happened to the horse and his confidence is growing by the second.

Hang on a minute

Natural instincts kick in and the horse decides to stop partway up the ramp. His attention is drawn away from the task. When the horse has stopped trying to face up to the job in hand, as this horse has, then the handler has to redirect his attention politely but firmly into the horsebox. This is where the horse needs to go and his mind must be kept on this objective. This can be achieved by asking the horse to bring his head round so he is looking into the horsebox.

Decision made!

The horse has been allowed the time to come to his own conclusions about the horsebox. He has not had any bad experiences and so has made up his own mind to enter. This conscious decision is crucial to the long-term success of the horse's training.

What normally happens when the horse reaches this point is that he is forced to go forward as people use lunge lines, brooms and whips on him, causing a great deal of tension and noise. As a result, a worried horse is coerced into going into the horsebox. Before going into the confined space the horse often fights back by rearing, running backwards, planting himself or plunging around. He is acting on his instincts but this is often misunderstood and the horse is reprimanded, verbally and/or physically. Consequently, the horse's natural fear of the horsebox is further heightened, and each loading becomes more difficult.

Now I'll take my time

Now that he's made it all the way into the horsebox and has been turned around, the horse can see that he does have a way out as well. Once again he needs time, help and encouragement to make the right decision to walk calmly down the ramp. All horses are individuals – some are claustrophobic, most act first and think later, some are much bolder than others. The important lesson is to let the horse have the time he needs to work out what he has to do.

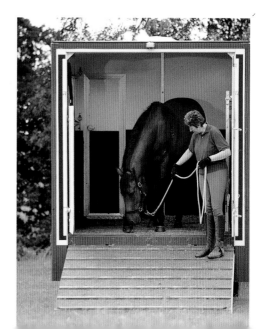

Easy does it

Here you can see the youngster coming down the ramp much more calmly, having learnt that there is no benefit to be gained by charging off.

DID YOU KNOW?

❏ Horses, like humans, adhere to decisions they have made themselves, but are not so committed to decisions that have been forced upon them in unpleasant circumstances. It is important to allow a horse time to decide that loading is safe.

I think it's time to go!

Unfortunately, a noise in the field behind suddenly startled this young horse and he shot out of the horsebox and leapt off from halfway down the ramp. If this happens, do not try to slow the horse down – in this instance, his natural instinct was to run from danger and hampering that would have increased his anxiety. The horse was allowed to calm down, loaded again and then unloaded. The next few times loading was attempted, he rushed down the ramp but was not restricted, and each time became slower.

On the road

Getting your horse into a trailer or horsebox is one thing, ensuring he travels well is another matter. The key to happy journeys lies very much in your hands, however. It is illegal to travel in the back of a trailer with your horse, but it's an enlightening experience. The ride is noisy, bumpy, scary at times, and physically and mentally demanding – and that is when the driver is considerate! The key points for drivers to remember are slow down, think ahead and allow plenty of time for manoeuvres.

Ready for anything

Kit out your horse in protective clothing when you transport him. The clothing has to be appropriate for the situation and the weather. Normally, when being transported by road, horses have protective legwear, which may cover their knees and hocks as well, and a tail bandage or guard. A poll guard may also be used to protect the top of the horse's head – a very vulnerable part of the body. A blow here in the right spot can be fatal. Rugs or sheets would be used according to the prevailing conditions. For safety, a leather headcollar should always be used as this does have a breaking point.

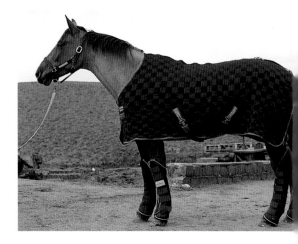

Claustrophobic or naughty?

Humans suffer claustrophobia and some horses also find confinement too much to bear. This is understandable when you consider that the ability to flee has ensured their survival, so being in a trailer or horsebox must be a major trial. Most horses find loading a challenge at first but, if treated correctly, they adapt easily. These horses, if driven considerately, accept travelling as well. However, if a horse displays extreme behaviour when travelling, this could be the result of a bad experience in the past or claustrophobia.

Due care and attention

Horses can be easy to load and calm travellers, but are likely to react badly if they experience inconsiderate driving. Driving a trailer well is an art and one that should be refined before any animals are carried in the trailer. Drivers have to accustom themselves to the length and breadth of the vehicle and trailer, especially when turning.

More room, more comfort

Horses generally travel better in lorries, as there is more room and they can balance more easily. The lorry driver must still be considerate and take special care if the horses are to remain willing travellers. When travelling, it is important to check the horses regularly. On a long journey, stops are recommended every couple of hours at which point it is a good idea to offer the horse a drink.

Index

aggression 26, 28, 64
  space problems 15
animals, reactions to 30–3,
  62–3
anxiety 18–19
  competitions 70–1
  leading 59, 66–7
  riding out 56–9
  training 76–9
apples 47
aromatherapy 71

Bach Flower Remedies 71
backing off 26
balls 50
barking dogs 31, 32, 63, 65
bars, stable 20, 51
bits 43
boldness 10
bolting 55
boredom 51
breaking in 55
breeding 34–5
bridling 41, 42
browbands 43
brushes 37
bucking 55, 80

calmness, rider's 78, 79
cars 57
catching a horse 24–5
cattle 33, 63
chewing
  rate of 50
  wood 51
chicken 33
claustrophobia 52–3, 90, 92
clipping 64
colour, health and 48
competitions 70–1
complementary therapies
  71, 81
concentration 72–3
confidence
  building 67
  entering trailers 88–91

jumping 84–7
confinement problems 52–3,
  88–91
cooling down 23
curiosity 27

discomfort 80–1
ditches 66, 84–5
dogs 31, 32, 63, 65
doors, rattling 65
dressage 82
driving trailers 93

ears 28–9
  reading 64
  touching 42, 43
eating 44–5
encouragement 74–5
endurance riding 71
exploring 18–21
eyes
  aggressiveness 28
  anxiousness 29

face pulling 36–7
family life 8
fear, training 76–9
feeding 44–5
feet, attention to 38, 39
female domination 9
fences, chewing 51
fields, new 21
fighting 12
first aid kits 93
flatwork 82–3
flehmen 29
flexibility 72
flight 12, 18, 63, 65
flooding 30, 63
foals 9, 34–5
  birth 9, 10
  feeding 35
  gangly legs 11, 34
  independence 35
following a horse 24
food 44–5, 47, 49

toys 50
frightened horses 56–9

games, group 16
gangly limbs 11, 34
girth 82
goats 33, 63
grass 44
grooming 36–9
  mutual 9
group living 8, 12, 13
  games 16
guard horses 12

hay 44, 50
heads, grooming 38
headshakers 69
healthy horses 46–9
heat 22
hedges 56
herds 8, 12, 13
  leader 9, 12
home, new 21
horse licks 51
horseboxes 88–93

inquisitiveness 20
insecurity, rider's 60, 61
instructors 61
isolation, diseases 46

jumping 70, 72, 80, 84–7

kicking out 37

labyrinth exercises 72
lead, following 10
leaders 9, 12
leading 59, 66–7
learning, play and 16
leg wear 92
lessons, concentration 72–3
lips 29
loading 88–91
lorries 93
  entering 19

mares
  dominance 9
  and foals 9, 34–55
medicines, in feed 45
memory 18
mental tiredness 73
mineral licks 45
mounting 54
mouths, touching 42, 43
mutual cooperation 8
mutual grooming 9
muzzles, sensitivity 21

neighbours 15, 20
nervous riders 60, 61
nervousness 63
  competitions 70–1
  leading 59, 66–7
  training 76–9
neuro-linguistic
  programming (NLP) 61
noises 63, 64–5, 91
nosebands 43

off-road riding 59

pace, setting 55
pain 80–1
pair bonding 13, 14–15
pigs 33
plastic bags 74, 77, 79
  walking on 73
playing 16–17
poles
  ground exercises 72
  jumping 72
poll guards 92
pregnancy 34
protective clothing,
  travelling 92
pulse rate 49
punishment 87

rattling doors 65
reacting to other animals
  30–3, 62–3
reacting to people 24–9
  being caught 24–5
  strangers 26–7

reacting to riders 60–1
reassurance 59, 74, 77
relaxation 82
reluctance 81
respiration rate 49
rewards 83
riders, response to 60
riding 54–67
road hazards 57–9, 63
rolling 21, 47
rubbing, rewards 74, 75, 83
rustling noises 77

saddles 40, 41, 55
scary objects 12, 18
scents 21
schooling 68–9, 82–3
separation anxiety 13
sexual games 17
shaking the head 69
sheep 33, 63
shoeing 78
sick horses 46–9
snapping 37
snow 23
socialization 8, 12, 13, 17
solitary life 13
sounds 63, 64–5, 77
spatial awareness 14, 15
  aggression 36
  memory 18
stables 36–53
  allocating 15
  claustrophobia 52–3
  feeding 44–5
  partition bars 20, 51
  toys 50–1
standing still 54
starting 55
strangers, reactions to 26–7
stress, competitions 70–1
stride, shortening 81
stroking 74, 75, 83
sunscreens 22
suppleness 69
survival mechanisms 12
suspicion 76
sweating 47
sweet itch 48

tack 40–3, 82
tail bandage 92
teachers 61
teeth 43
Tellington-Touch Equine
  Awareness Method
  (TTEAM) 42, 43
temperature 49
throwing up the head 69
tiredness 73
touch 9
towing hazards 58
toys 50–1
traffic 56–9
trailers 53, 88–93
training 68–87
transporting 88–93
travelling 88–93
trec 71
turning 69

unexpected 57–8, 74
unloading 88–91

vets 81

walkers, reaction to 26–7, 56
wariness 76
warm-ups 68, 69
warning 15
water 49
  fear of 77
  travelling 93
weaning 34
weather 22–3, 68
wind 22
windsucking 44
wood, chewing 51
worried horses 12, 18–19
writhing 47

young horses
  boldness 10
  handling 37
  mental tiredness 73
  play 16–17
  training 68–87

Acknowledgements

Executive editor Trevor Davies
Editor Rachel Lawrence
Executive art editor Leigh Jones
Designer Louise Griffiths
Picture researcher Zoë Holterman
Production controller Edward Carter
Special photography Bob Atkins

Photographic Acknowledgements
All photography © Octopus Publishing Group Limited / Bob Atkins except for
the following listed below:
Bruce Coleman Collection / Robert Maier 23 bottom left.
Your Horse Magazine / Emap Active Ltd. 33 right, 52, 53 top, 53 bottom, 55 top,
59 bottom, 61, 70 left, 70 right, 71 left, 71 right, 80 left, 80 right, 81 top, 81 bottom,
92 left, 92 right, 93 left, 93 right.